LIFE ON A CATTLE FARM

LIFE ON A CATTLE FARM

by Judy Wolfman
photographs by David Lorenz Winston

LIFE ON A
FARM

Carolrhoda Books, Inc. / Minneapolis

Our thanks and appreciation to Gary and Adam Smith for your cooperation and patience in helping us tell your story. We couldn't have done it without you!　　　—J.W. and D.L.W.

Thanks to the Pennsylvania Beef Council for providing additional information on beef cattle.
　　　—J.W.

Carolrhoda Books, Inc.
A division of Lerner Publishing Group
241 First Avenue North
Minneapolis, MN 55401 U.S.A.

Website address: www.lernerbooks.com

LIBRARY OF CONGRESS CATALOGING-IN-PUBLICATION DATA

Wolfman, Judy.
　　Life on a cattle farm / by Judy Wolfman ; photographs by David Lorenz Winston.
　　　　p.　　cm. — (Life on a farm)
　　Includes index.
　　ISBN 1-57505-516-3 (lib. bdg. : alk. paper)
　1. Beef cattle—Juvenile literature. 2. Cows—Juvenile literature. 3. Farm life—Juvenile literature. [1. Beef cattle. 2. Cattle. 3. Farm life.] I. Title. II. Winston, David Lorenz, ill. III. Series.
SF207.W58　2002
636.2'22—dc21　　　　　　　　　　　　00-010626

Manufactured in the United States of America
1 2 3 4 5 6 – JR – 07 06 05 04 03 02

CONTENTS

WELCOME

to our Farm

I take a break with my dog, Teal, in front of the cattle barn.

My friends think I'm one of the luckiest boys they know. Why? Because I live on a beef cattle farm, where I can look out my window and see beautiful cows and peaceful pastures. And even better, I get to spend hours outside with our animals every day.

I'm Adam Smith, and I've lived here all my life. My dad grew up on a dairy farm. Dairy cattle are raised to provide milk for people. They have to be milked twice a day. Dad loved cattle, but he didn't love all that milking. After my grandpa died, Dad decided to run his own beef cattle farm. Beef cattle are raised for meat, so we don't have to milk them.

Cow experts think that the brown patches around a Hereford's eyes help keep flies away.

Our cattle are **polled** Herefords. (Polled cattle are born without horns.) Herefords are reddish-brown animals with pretty white faces. There are many kinds of beef cattle in the United States, but we like polled Herefords best. They're calm, friendly, and easy to raise. Their meat is tasty and not too fatty.

8

About fifty cows live on our farm.

Our bull weighs close to 2,000 pounds. That's almost as big as a small car!

We have about twenty **cows**, or female cattle. We don't sell the cows for meat. They're kept on the farm to have babies, or **calves**. We also have a **bull**, or a male. We use him to **breed** the cows so that they'll have calves. In the middle of June, we turn the bull loose in the pasture to run with the herd. He sniffs the cows to find out which ones are in **heat** and ready to mate. We hope he'll breed lots of them!

This cow is pregnant. We try to time each cow's breeding so that her calf will be born in early spring, when the weather is warm enough for the calf to do well.

It's hard to know if a cow is pregnant. A full-grown cow weighs at least 1,000 pounds. Cows are so big that at first, a pregnant one doesn't look any different than normal. Dad and I try to tell by **bumping** each cow, or hitting her gently along the side. The calf has usually been growing inside the cow for three or four months before we can feel it.

To make sure the calves will be born strong, we give the mothers salt and minerals mixed in with their feed. The cows like the taste, and it helps them stay healthy. We also give each pregnant cow a shot to protect the calf from disease.

11

Like a human mother, a cow carries her baby for nine months. In the early spring, the cow is ready to give birth. She leaves the herd and goes off by herself.

Usually, she has the baby on her own, without help from us. Sometimes we don't even know a cow has given birth until we see the calf.

A mother cow licks her newborn calf.

This calf is just about clean.

Most calves are born front feet first with their eyes open. The calf is covered with a slimy substance called **mucus**, which the mother licks off. The newborn calf is very tired. It sleeps for a while, then wakes up and tries to stand. It's very shaky and falls a lot at first. But before long, it can walk to its mom to **nurse**, or drink milk from her body.

This calf is just one day old.

A hungry calf nurses from its mother.

Once in a while, the calf comes out backward. This is dangerous, because the calf can get stuck—and it needs air right away. So Dad and I spring into action. We tie a chain or rope around the calf's back feet. Then we pull as hard and fast as we can to get the calf out quickly. A calf weighs almost 100 pounds and is about the size of a German shepherd, so it's not easy to pull out.

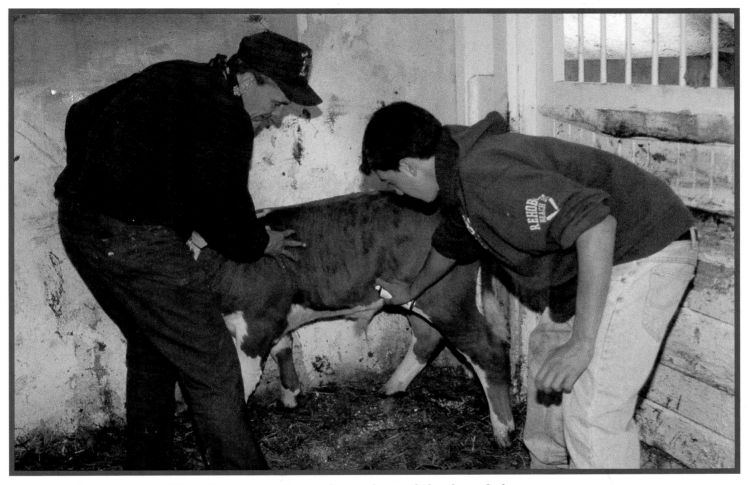

Dad and I spray a calf's belly with iodine to keep the umbilical cord clean.

Soon after the birth, the **umbilical cord** breaks. This cord is like a lifeline. While the calf grows inside its mother, it gets its food and oxygen through the cord. When the cord breaks, a small piece is left behind on the calf's stomach. Dad and I spray it with iodine to prevent infection. In a few days, it dries up. Eventually it falls off.

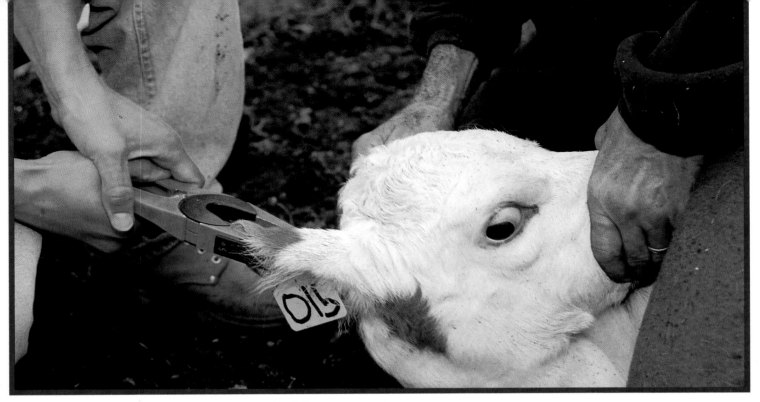

This calf is 015. That means it was the fifteenth cow born in 2000.

We give each calf a number so we can tell the animals apart. When a calf is a few days old, we clip a tag with the number to the calf's ear. The first part of the number comes from the year of the calf's birth. For calves born in 2001, the first part of the number is 1. For 1999, it's 9. The second part of a calf's number comes from the order of its birth that year. The first calf born in 2001 was number 101, and the second was 102. The first calf born in 1999 was 901.

Since the tag is on the outside of the calf's ear, it's easy to see. But it could fall off and get lost. So we also tattoo the calf's number in its other ear. The tattoo ink never wears off. As the calf grows, the number grows with it, so it can always be seen.

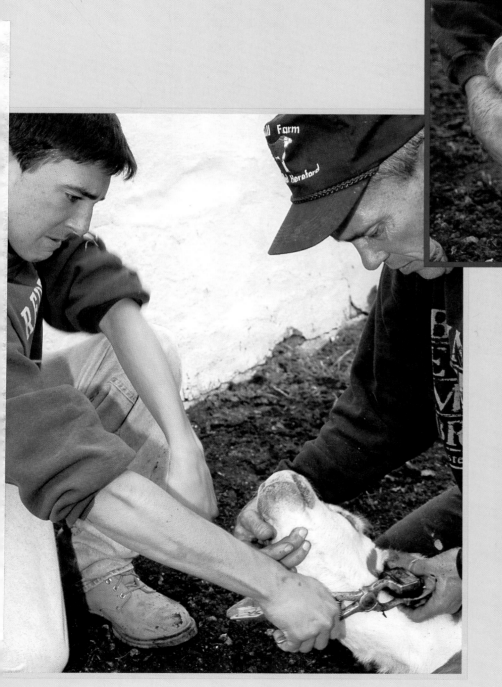

First we spread ink in the calf's ear. Then we use a tool to tattoo the calf's number into the ear.

We can change the numbers on this tool, so we can use it to tattoo every calf.

17

Most calves stay healthy as they grow. But every once in a while, one catches a terrible disease called scours. A calf with scours gets a high fever and diarrhea. It will die within a day and a half if we don't treat it. The rest of the calves could catch the disease, too. So Dad and I are always on the lookout.

We walk through the herd, looking for white **manure** or a white area on a calf's rump. We also look for any calf that hangs its head and lets its ears droop. If we find a sick calf, we give it a pill right away. The calf usually gets well within about half a day.

Lucky for us, most of our calves are as healthy and happy as these.

A calf gets both food and a substance that fights germs from its mother's milk.

Diseases like scours are rare. But to help our calves stay healthy, we watch over them and keep their umbilical cord clean. We also keep them out of the mud so they won't get wet and catch a cold.

The mother cows help, too. A cow's milk is the perfect food for her calf because it contains **colostrum.** Colostrum helps a calf fight off germs, so nursing is very good for it.

A cow usually has just one calf at a time. She'll live fifteen years or so, so she'll have about fourteen or fifteen calves in her lifetime.

We can tell when a calf wants to nurse by its cry. They're just like babies! Their moo is so loud that it sounds like a roar—like they're saying, "Hey, Mom, I'm *hungry!*" Each cow knows her calf's voice. If the calf is young, the cow follows the cry until she reaches the calf. Then the calf nurses for as long as it wants.

But as the calf gets older, the mom starts to ignore its cries. She seems to be saying, "Come on, now, you know how to take care of yourself. I'm over here. If you want to eat, you come to me." The calf keeps crying, but before long it goes to its mom.

Cows and calves communicate in many ways.
This cow is using her tail to stay in touch with her calf.

A cow and a calf enjoy
a quiet rest together.

A rare visit between a calf and its dad.
Our bull only sees the calves when we
let him run loose with the herd.

That's how life begins for a polled Hereford calf. For the next few months, the calf's job is to grow, the cow's job is to take care of the calf, and our job is to take care of all them—which means a lot of work.

Calves grow quickly. By the time this calf is nine months old, it will weigh at least 600 pounds.

I use a pitchfork to fill a trough with hay for the cows.

On the JOB

On a cattle farm, there's always something to do. For one thing, we have to keep the animals fed. Pregnant cows and older calves eat a feed mixture made of corn, minerals, and salt. These ingredients are ground with molasses to make the feed taste sweet. We put feed in the troughs in the barn once a day. The cattle eat whenever they're hungry. Cows that aren't pregnant eat grass in the warm months and hay in the winter, so feeding them is less work.

Cattle are born with small bottom teeth. They have no top front teeth at all, just a hard gum. So a cow doesn't chew the way a person does. It crunches down on its food and grinds it by moving its mouth in circles. After a cow swallows, the food sits in its stomach for a few minutes. Then the cow brings it up as **cud** and chews it again. Chewing the cud makes it easier for the animal's stomach to process the food.

The cattle line up for a meal during feeding time in the barn.

Of course, the cattle need water, too. They have their own drinking fountains inside and outside the barn. Any time they're thirsty, they can get a drink. The fountains never freeze, so the cows can get water even in the winter.

The cattle stay out in the pasture day and night. But they know the way to the barn and are free to go in and out. In winter, when snow is on the ground, they usually go in the barn to stay warm and dry. And when it's too hot in the summer, the cattle go inside, where the barn's stone walls help keep them cool.

Our barn holds all fifty cows on the farm.

First, Dad uses the tractor to scoop the manure from the floor of the barn.

Then I fork the manure into the spreader. We scatter the manure in our field to help the hay grow.

I'm not too happy when the cattle spend a lot of time in the barn. The barn's floor is covered with a layer of hay, and the cattle leave their droppings all over it. They make quite a mess— and Dad and I have to clean it up! But thanks to our tractor, the job's not too bad. We just scoop up the manure and take it out to spread in the field, where it helps our hay grow. Then we put new hay on the barn floor.

28

The cows will always follow me to the barn if I have a bucket of feed!

Fly control is another big job in spring and summer. Flies can give cattle a disease called pinkeye. When tall grass makes a cow's eyes water, flies land on the eyes and carry germs into them. Pinkeye makes a cow's eyes red, crusty, and sticky—just like it does in people. And it spreads quickly from one animal to another. So every spring, Dad and I start Operation Fly Control.

First, in April, we give every cow and calf a shot. We start by rounding up the cattle and bringing them to the barn. The hardest part is catching them! One way I help is by filling my white bucket with feed. The cattle follow me, hoping to get something to eat.

Dad and I herd the cattle into the barn. We close the gate so they can't get out. Then we herd each cow into a stall and put it into a headlock to hold it still. We give the cow a shot to prevent pinkeye and clip a tag on its ear. The tag contains a chemical that keeps flies away.

The green tag contains a chemical that flies don't like, so they stay away from the cow.

A cow's tail is strong and bends easily, so it's a good tool for swatting flies away. We hope the sticky strips will catch lots of flies, too.

Operation Fly Control has a few other steps. Dad and I cut the grass often to keep it low. We spray the barn to kill flies. Then we hang sticky strips to catch any that survive. And every three weeks, we pour a special liquid on the cattle to keep the flies away.

The cattle help themselves, too. They chase flies away with their long tail. But if a cow or calf does get pinkeye, we take it away from the rest of the herd and give it some medicine. The disease takes a few weeks to clear up. Until it does, the animal must stay by itself so that it won't infect the other cows.

Dad and I have to keep an eye on the fence to make sure it's always sturdy.
If a cow escapes, it could get lost or wander to the road and get hit by a car.

Besides taking care of the cattle, there are lots of other things to do on the farm. We have a fence around our 40 acres of pasture to keep the cows in. Sometimes the cows bump the fence and weaken it. If we don't fix it, the cows could knock it down and get out. So Dad and I walk along the fence often. We look for weak spots and repair them.

We also grow our own hay. That way, we don't have to spend money buying it. In the spring, I use the tractor to break up the ground and plant seeds. The hay grows for several months. We use a machine to cut it, and it dries for a few days. Then I drive another machine that rakes the hay and gets it ready to be baled.

One of my jobs is to rake the hay from the field. Our machines save us a lot of work with the hay. I'm glad I wasn't a farmer back in the days when everything had to be done by hand!

Here I am stacking the baled hay. A bale of hay weighs between 30 and 40 pounds. It's a good thing I have strong arms!

The baler is great to watch. It gathers up the hay, packs it into a bale, ties it, then shoots it onto a wagon. When the wagon is full, we take it to the barn and unload the bales.

When I'm not working on the farm, I like to ride my dirt bike and hang out with my friends.

Sometimes my friends come over to help us with the hay or other jobs. None of them live on a farm, so they think it's cool to work on one. Dad pays them for their help, too. When we're done with our chores, he lets us ride our dirt bikes through the woods and fields. It's a great way to end a hard day's work!

A mother cow moos for her calf, which is on the other side of the fence.

CATTLE
for Sale

All summer long, the calves get bigger and bigger. By December, they've been nursing since March or April. Each calf weighs 600 to 800 pounds. The mother cows are usually pregnant again. They need to rest and get ready for the new babies that will be born in a few months. So we **wean** the calves, or separate them from their mothers so that they'll stop nursing.

After a while, weaned calves get used to being with each other instead of their moms.

Dad and I herd the calves and the cows into two big stalls in the barn. For two or three days, the barn is a noisy place. The calves moo for their moms. It sounds like a bunch of vans are roaring through the barn. But the calves like the feed we give them, and they calm down before long.

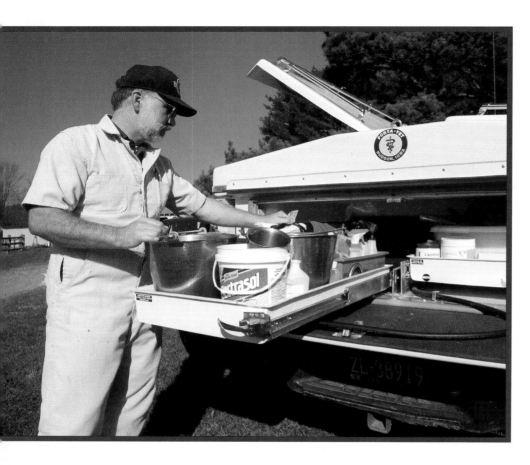

Dr. Marshall, our veterinarian, brings medical supplies with him in his truck. That way, the cattle don't have to leave the farm until they're sold.

Once the cattle are weaned, we can start getting ready to sell them. The females who haven't had calves yet are called **heifers.** Sometimes we keep a heifer to replace a cow that's gotten old or sick. But we sell most of them. Their new owners use them for breeding.

We also sell the young bulls, which are used for meat. A few months before a bull is sold, a veterinarian operates on it to remove its testicles. (Testicles are male body parts that are important for breeding.) After a bull has had this operation, it's called a **steer.** Without testicles, steers get bigger muscles, so they provide more meat.

A large, healthy steer runs along the fence.

My dad and a buyer discuss the price of a steer.

Buyers who are interested in our cattle like to visit the farm. They look at the herd and see how we raise our calves. This way, they know our cattle are healthy. A cattle buyer looks for a steer or heifer that stands straight and has a straight back with no hump. The animal shouldn't be too skinny or too big. Buyers also like to see an animal's parents. If the parents are strong and healthy, the steer or heifer probably is, too.

40

I don't get too attached to the cattle, so when one leaves us, I'm not sad. Selling cattle is our business. It's what keeps the farm going. I like knowing that our animals are going to a new home where they'll breed calves or provide good food for a family.

Even though I don't mind selling the steers and heifers, I do like being with our cows. There's something about them that calms me down, even if I'm in a bad mood. My favorite cow is 002. (She was the second one born in 1990.) She's old and gentle. She likes to sniff me and nuzzle my hands. Her tongue is rough, almost like sandpaper, but it doesn't hurt.

I like being in the fields with our cows. Here I'm feeding my favorite cow, who eats right out of my hand.

Living on a beef cattle farm is an exciting and fun way to grow up. I don't mind most of the hard work, like fixing fences and baling hay. Even cleaning out the smelly barn isn't so bad. I like spending time with the animals and taking care of them. I like looking out my window and seeing the pasture and the cows. I like driving the tractor. I'm not sure about what I'll do in the future, but it's hard to think of anything better than staying right here on our farm.

Fun Facts about CATTLE

HAVE YOU EVER HEARD OF A BEEFALO? This unusual farm animal is a cross between cattle and bison, which are often called buffalo. Beefalo farmers say that the animal's meat is delicious and not as fatty as beef.

In the Hindu religion, the cow is a sacred animal. Hindus do not eat beef, and Hindu law forbids the harming of cattle.

In 1493, Christopher Columbus brought cattle from Spain to the West Indies on his second voyage across the Atlantic Ocean.

Spain

West Indies

More than 13 million beef cattle live in Texas. That's more than in any other state.

Texas is also famous for the Texas longhorn, a type of beef cattle with large horns. The biggest set of horns ever measured on a longhorn spanned 9 feet!

Scientists believe that cattle had a huge wild ancestor called the aurochs. A bull aurochs stood 6½ feet tall at the shoulder. That's as tall as a very tall human adult!

People use cattle in more ways than any other farm animal. Cattle provide **BEEF, MILK, LEATHER, FERTILIZER,** and **GLUE.** In many parts of the world, cattle also work by pulling carts and plows.

Learn More about CATTLE

Books

Cooper, Jason. *Beef.* Vero Beach, FL: Rourke Publications, 1997. This photo book shows how beef is processed, from the farm to the grocery stores where people shop.

Patent, Dorothy Hinshaw. *Cattle.* Minneapolis: Carolrhoda Books, 1993. How do cattle live and grow? How do they help people? Find out about all kinds of cattle and their relatives in this photo book.

Thomas, Heather Smith. *Your Calf: A Kid's Guide to Raising and Showing Beef and Dairy Calves.* Williamstown, MA: Storey Books, 1997. For the young farmer interested in showing a calf at a fair, this book has detailed information on how to keep cattle healthy and happy.

Websites

Cows of the World
<http://www.allcows.com/world/index3.htm>
This cattle lover's site features facts about and photographs of twenty-four kinds of beef and dairy cattle, including Herefords and Texas longhorns.

Hereford Cattle Society
<http://www.ibmpcug.co.uk/~mserve/herdsoc.html>
Learn about the different types of Herefords and their history at the official website of this English cattle organization.

Rollins Cattle Company
<http://www.alltel.net/~bonnie5/watusi001.htm>
Visit a North Carolina farm and meet an unusual type of beef cattle—the Watusi.

45

GLOSSARY

breed: to make pregnant

bulls: male cattle that can breed

bumping: gently hitting female cattle on the side to find out if they are pregnant

calves: baby cattle

colostrum: a liquid in a cow's milk that helps a newborn calf stay healthy

cows: female cattle. (The word *cow* can also mean any single cattle, male or female.)

cud: food that cattle bring up from the stomach to chew a second time

heat: the time when a female animal can become pregnant

heifers: young female cattle that have not given birth

manure: animal droppings

mucus: a slimy substance that covers a newborn calf

nurse: to drink milk from a mother's body

polled: born without horns

steers: male cattle that have had an operation to remove the testicles. Steers cannot breed.

umbilical cord: the lifeline that connects a mother and baby while the baby grows inside the mother

wean: to separate a young animal from its mother so that it will begin to eat solid food

 # INDEX

About the AUTHOR

Judy Wolfman is a writer and professional storyteller who presents workshops on creativity and storytelling. She also enjoys both acting and writing for the theater. Her published works include children's plays, numerous magazine articles, and Carolrhoda's Life on a Farm series. A retired schoolteacher, she has two sons, a daughter, and four granddaughters. She lives in York, Pennsylvania.

About the PHOTOGRAPHER

David Lorenz Winston is an award-winning photographer whose work has been published by *National Geographic World,* UNICEF, and the National Wildlife Federation. In addition to his work on the Life on a Farm series, Mr. Winston has been photographing pigs, cows, and other animals for many years. He lives in southeastern Pennsylvania. To learn more about Mr. Winston's work, visit his website at <http://www.davidlorenzwinston.com>.